This book belongs to

....

To my first best friend, Pepper. To the staff and dogs at Oakwood Dog Rescue and to all the incredible dogs around the world.—KL

Published in 2023 by Welbeck Editions
An imprint of Welbeck Children's Limited,
part of the Welbeck Publishing Group
Offices in: London – 20 Mortimer Street, London W1T 3JW
& Sydney – Level 17, 207 Kent St, Sydney NSW 2000 Australia

www.welbeckpublishing.com

Design and layout © Welbeck Children's Limited
Text & illustrations © 2023 Kristyna Litten

Art Director: Margaret Hope
Senior Editor: Jenni Lazell

978 1 80338 112 1

Printed in Heshan, China

10 9 8 7 6 5 4 3 2 1

AROUND THE WORLD IN 80 DOGS

KRISTYNA LITTEN

WELBECK
EDITIONS

Contents

Dhole

Coyote

Arctic Fox

Red Fox

Ethiopian Wolf

Bat-Eared Dog

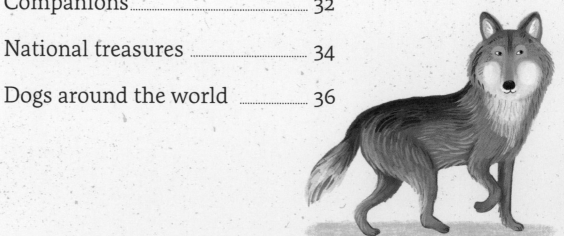

Grey Wolf

Maned Wolf

Tibetan Fox

Fennec

African Wild Dog

Jackal

Bush Dog

Tanuki-Racoon Dog

Domestic Dog

A world of dogs

Dogs are one of our closest animal companions. They have traveled alongside us to every continent on Earth.

They may have started out as wary wolves, coming close to score some easy food but, over thousands of years, dogs have evolved into the most diverse mammal on the planet and are involved in almost every part of our lives.

They protect us, hunt with us, and help us travel. They can guide us, find us, and get us through the toughest of times.

No matter whether they're sprinting across sandy deserts, blazing through blizzards, trotting through towns, or simply snuggling up on the sofa—dogs are here to stay. Right by our side.

It's time to grab the leash, pack some poop bags, and discover the wonderful world of dogs!

Like me!

And me!

A tail of time: The evolution of man's best friend

The gray wolf

Twenty million years ago, canines and felines branched into two separate families. One ancestor to the wolf, the Tomarctus, lived over 15 million years ago. It developed pads on its feet, and a fifth toe (the dew claw)—features we see on dogs and wolves today. The oldest living relative of the dogs we know today is the gray wolf, with which domestic dogs share 98.8% of their DNA.

(canis lupus)

Modern human

Originated in Africa 200,000 years ago.

(Homo sapien)

Domestication of wolves

Though we do not know exactly where, when or how domestication began, most theories suggest it happened in Eurasia between 15,000 and 40,000 years ago.

It's likely that some wolves partially domesticated themselves, following human hunters and becoming less fearful of them. Friendlier wolves may have received scraps and decided to live closer to humans, guarding their new food source and working together.

The earliest evidence of dogs and humans living together comes from fossils dating back over 14,000 years.

Domesticated dogs

Over many generations, the characteristics, appearance, and genetics of these wolves began to change, becoming a new subspecies—*canis lupus familiaris.*

Ancient artifacts

Rock carvings and ancient pottery showing dogs dates back over 8,000 years, telling us dogs were important to early societies.

Now and forever

Dogs are a huge part of our lives. They are social media superstars and science superheroes, and they will continue to surprise us as human's best friend.

Agriculture

Humans developed settlements, grew food, and began domesticating other animals like goats, sheep, and cattle over 10,000 years ago. Dogs protected and helped move the flocks.

On the move

Dog remains found in Russia suggest people have used dogs for sledding for at least 9,500 years. The oldest of this type of dog originated in Siberia, and the Greenland dog is its closest living relative.

Five types

It is believed that ancient Egyptians were the first to breed dogs for specific purposes. By 6,000 years ago there were five distinct types of domestic dog: Mastiffs, Spitz, sight hounds, pointing dogs, and herding dogs.

Canine colleagues

Dogs have been given more and more responsibilities, from search and rescue to police dogs. We trust them with our lives.

Dogs in space, 1957

Companion canines

Around 2,000 years ago, people of nobility began breeding dogs as companions and status symbols.

The last 200 years

Most of the breeds we know today were developed over the last 200 years. Humans selectively bred dogs not only for hunting and guarding but also for their appearance. Today, there are well over 400 breeds of dog.

Ancient dogs

Most of the dog breeds we know today have only existed in the last 200 to 300 years, but some have been around for thousands of years. Prehistoric cave paintings and studies of ancient remains can give us an idea of when and where some of these first dogs existed.

Iranian pottery that is 8,000-year-old shows dogs thought to be the Saluki or the Afghan Hound.

1. Saluki (Middle East)

For at least 5,000 years, Salukis have been treasured for their elegance, unmatched speed, and hunting skills. They were even considered worthy enough to be mummified and buried alongside ancient Egyptian pharaohs, and are still considered to be the royal dog of Egypt. While as fast as the wind, peaceful, sensitive Salukis would much rather snooze on the couch.

2. Akita Inu (Japan)

Once a badge of status, wealth, and aristocracy, ownership of an Akita was, until the 19th century, restricted to royalty and samurai, who used the dogs to guard them while they slept. Akitas are so strong and hardy they were once used to trap bears, holding them at bay until hunters came. But they are best known for their fierce loyalty thanks to one dog, Hachikō, and his story of unwavering devotion to his owner. You can spot statues of Hachikō throughout Tokyo.

3. Tibetan Mastiff (Tibet)

To get hold of a Tibetan Mastiff you'll need a wallet the size of this dog's head—and that's pretty huge! Thought to be the oldest (3,000 years) and most rare type of Mastiff, this gigantic guardian dog is the most expensive dog in the world. For this reason they are seen as a symbol of wealth: one Mastiff with red fur sold for $1.9 million in 2014. Bred to guard livestock, this bearlike fluffy giant is always on the alert for potential intruders.

4. Basenji (Africa)

The Basenji is an ancient breed whose unique features are down to nature, instead of human involvement. Though known as the barkless dog, Basenjis are far from silent – instead of barking, they yodel! Known to be smart and independent, these energetic curly-tailed hunters were used by African tribes for thousands of years to lure lions, attaching bells to their dog's collars to make them easier to find.

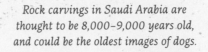

Rock carvings in Saudi Arabia are thought to be 8,000–9,000 years old, and could be the oldest images of dogs.

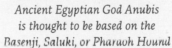

Ancient Egyptian God Anubis is thought to be based on the Basenji, Saluki, or Pharaoh Hound

5. Afghan Hound (Afghanistan)

Surely such a fabulously silky-haired hound like the Afghan has always been strutting its stuff elegantly down a catwalk! In fact, as a breed dating back over 3,000 years, they were once tenacious hunters, known to take on snarly snow leopards and fast-moving antelope. Their long hair was ideal for keeping them warm in the bitterly cold Afghan nights and their large feet helped them leap easily at high speed across the harsh mountain terrain.

Statues of Chows called "foo dogs" are still seen outside temples, palaces, and even outside restaurants.

6. Chow Chow (China)

With fur so dense you could almost get lost in it, it's no surprise that the Chinese call this the "Puffy Lion Dog." Chows even have a thick ruff of fur around the neck like a lion's mane. For at least 2,000 years, they have symbolized protection, wealth, and success. One emperor of the Tang Dynasty had a whopping 5,000, some of which would have been used to guard temples.

Great guardians

When humans began to domesticate other animals, such as goats and sheep, they used these dogs' natural guarding instincts to help protect the livestock from wild predators, such as wolves, coyotes, and foxes. These large watchdogs lived alongside the flock, often staying with them day and night.

7. Caucasian Shepherd Dog
(Georgia, Armenia, Azerbaijan)

Given this breed's colossal size, power, and thick, furry coat, it is no surprise that they were sometimes mistaken for the bears they were originally hunting. Their highly territorial nature and strength made them ideal for protecting flock, and many were later recruited as Russian guard dogs.

8. Maremma (Italy)

When it comes to guarding, this gentle giant considers the flock their family. Some of these big dogs are even used to save the population of one of the world's smallest penguin species. Living on a small Australian island, the appropriately named Little penguins were in big trouble from foxes before a Maremma called Oddball came to their rescue. Thanks to Maremma dogs, there are now many more penguins on the island.

9. Bakharwal (India)

High in the Himalayan mountains lives one of India's most ancient dogs. The Bakharwal has lived alongside north Indian tribes for many years as a watchdog for their settlements and livestock. They have adapted to the high altitudes and harsh climate with their thick coat and unusual vegetarian diet of bread, milk, and maize.

Thanks for keeping me safe while I chomp this grass.

10. Great Pyrenees (France, Spain)

This nocturnal fluffy white breed was originally used to guard sheep at night. Their color and size allowed them to blend perfectly into the flock, disguising them from predators. The Pyrenees were so good at their job that, in the 17th century, they were adopted by French royals to guard manor houses and palaces, and are still considered the royal dog of France.

A brave Pyrenees called Odin refused to leave his goats during a wildfire. When the family returned, their home and property was completely destroyed. But Odin aproached them, having saved not only all of the goats but a fleeing group of deer as well. What a hero!

That's a funny-looking sheep.

Sprightly shepherds

As humans began living in settlements, some dogs were used to help move livestock from place to place. These breeds learned to make problem-solving decisions quickly, which has made shepherd dogs like these some of the smartest dogs around.

11. Bernese Mountain Dog
(Switzerland)

Smiley "Berners" make fantastic all-around farm dogs. Not only do they move and guard cattle but, because they are capable of pulling up to ten times their weight, pulling carts full of produce to market was also part of their job description. The produce was often milk and cheese, earning them the nickname "cheese dogs" in their local area. Today, their sweet, affectionate nature and big bear hugs make them very popular therapy dogs.

Say cheese!

12. Mudi (Hungary)

Hungary is a nation of shepherd dogs. Large ones, such as the Komondor and Kuvasz, are often used to guard, while smaller ones like the Mudi, Puli, and Pumi, drive and control the flock. Mudis are barely seen outside their native country, but are greatly prized among Hungarian shepherds. This small shepherd breed loves to have a job and can lend a paw to almost any activity, from sports to detection and search and rescue, taking any responsibility very seriously.

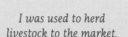

I was used to herd livestock to the market.

I worked in the fields, where my long fur protected me from extreme weather

13. Collie (Scotland)

There are a few breeds that share the name Collie, such as the Border and Bearded Collie. They are all herding dogs. The standard Collie comes in two types: rough coated and smooth coated. They were relatively unheard of until popularized by Queen Victoria in the 19th century, and then further by the movie and TV show *Lassie*, which highlighted the faithfulness of this affectionate breed.

Rough Collie

Smooth Collie

14. Australian Cattle Dog (Australia)

Also known by the name Heeler because of they way they move cattle (by nipping at their heels), this brainy breed is a magnificent mix of native Kelpie, Collie and Dalmation, with a dash of Dingo. They are energetic, intelligent, and very loyal to their families. One of the oldest dogs in the world was a working Heeler named Bluey, who lived to 29 years old.

Scentsational smell

The sniffer, the snoot, the schnozzle, the boop button. Whatever you call it, a dog's nose is incredible. It's how they "see" the world. With their nose they can detect, recognize, and follow specific scents, which is why we use them for tracking, hunting, and finding just about anything we need them to.

A dog's nose is ...

🐾 Up to 100,000 times more powerful than a human's.

🐾 As unique as a fingerprint.

🐾 Cold to the touch, as they act as a super-sensitive heat detector.

🐾 Wet to help absorb scent chemicals.

And as if that wasn't awesome enough ... dogs don't have just one nose, but two! Their second "nose" (called the vomeronasal organ) is found on the roof of their mouth and used to analyze smells and help them communicate with their furry friends.

Beryl

**Top six
super sniffer breeds**

1. Bloodhound
2. Basset Hound
3. Beagle
4. German Shepherd
5. Labrador Retriever
6. Belgian Malinois

The nose with the paws

A Bloodhound's long, droopy ears and wrinkly skin may look silly but they are specifically designed to help collect the odor molecules and sweep them toward their nose. They can trail a scent that could be up to 12 days old over a distance of 130 miles.

Sniffing each other's bums is an important greeting and it's how dogs gather information about one another. It's the doggy equivalent of looking at someone's online profile.

DOGGY IDENTITY CARD

NAME
BERYL
AGE
3 YEARS
RELATIONSHIP STATUS
SINGLE
LAST MEAL
CHICKEN AND RICE

234587

Hey Derek!
I thought it was you!

Can dogs smell our feelings?

There is no hiding how we feel from our dogs because they CAN smell it. Not only can they smell and understand our emotions, but they react to them, too. When we are happy, certain chemicals are released into our bloodstream, and dogs often respond with a happy wagging tail. However, if we express fear, dogs also show signs of stress. So if it's movie night, your dog's choice would be a rom-com over a horror film every time.

Can dogs smell time?

Ever wondered how dogs know exactly when to wait by the door, wagging their tails before you walk in? It could be that magnificent nose again. Seven am will smell completely different to six pm to a dog. This is because when we leave our home we leave our scent. Throughout the day that scent fades with every hour, acting like a canine clock.

My nose tells me it's treat time.

Truffle hunting is the oldest use of detection in dogs. People used the ancient Italian Lagotto Romagnolo because of their acute scenting powers.

Allergy detection dogs can alert their owner when they scent allergens, such as peanuts, before their owner comes into contact with them. They often wear a vest indicating where to find medication in case of an emergency.

Medical detection dogs are saving lives. Tangle the Spaniel showed that because dogs can smell minute scent changes, they can be used to diagnose all sorts of illnesses much earlier. This is an invaluable skill that scientists are trying to recreate with a mechanical dog Robot Nose.

Medical alert dogs can sense and communicate to their owner that they may need to take certain medical actions. For example, a dog can sense a change in blood sugar levels in someone who has diabetes and indicate that they may need insulin. In other cases, a dog can be trained to detect an impending seizure sometimes up to 45 minutes beforehand, and make sure their owner gets to safety.

Some dogs sniff hives to make sure bees and their honey are safe.

Scent tracking dogs are playing a vital role in environmental science. To study the decline of whales and dolphins, scientists must find scat (whale poop) in the water, in order to analyze its DNA. This would be an almost impossible task if it wasn't for dogs who can indicate to their handlers where to find whale poop up to a mile away.

Working woofers
Police pups and military mutts

My job would be impossible without my canine coworker.

15. English Springer Spaniel (England)

The Springer Spaniel is the perfect student. Eager to learn, spring into action, and get the job done. Because of this high energy and willingness to please, the Field English Springer Spaniel is the most popular detection specialist dog, used by police to check baggage, containers, and vehicles.

The best student award goes to a dog named Scamp. In just a few years he found over $7.5 million worth of illegal substances. He was so good at his job, criminal gangs wanted to track him down.

16. Bloodhound (England)

Way before detectives were able to use DNA evidence, dogs were sniffing out clues and catching criminals. It's no surprise that the Bloodhound is referred to as the "Detective dog." Originally used to hunt boar and deer, they were soon tasked to track down thieves and outlaws. But their importance to law enforcement doesn't end there—evidence found by this incredible dog's nose is so reliable, it can be used in court and help bring people to justice.

You've done it again! I would never have solved this crime without the clues you found.

K9-UNIT

I know a dog that won a medal for saving endangered rhinos from poachers!

17. Belgian Malinois (Belgium)

Mission impawssible? Not for the Malinois, who is fast, highly agile, smart, and obedient. Some can even hold their breath under water, run up walls, and walk blindfolded across tightropes, making them the perfect candidate as a Multipurpose Canine (MPC). These are military dogs selectively trained for special operations. Only one percent of military dogs pass the training and go on to work on secret missions, where they may need to parachute, track people or explosives, and even get involved in combat.

All Beagles have a white tipped tail, which people once used to help identify them in long grass.

18. Beagle (United Kingdom)

Just like the super snoot of the Bloodhound, the bouncy Beagle's nose can determine specific scents, and they won't stop until their job is done. This makes them a wonderful working dog. It is the job for teams of Beagles, called the Beagle Brigade, to sniff out and alert their handler to any illegal substances, such as drugs and explosives, or even bedbugs, at airports.

Search and rescue

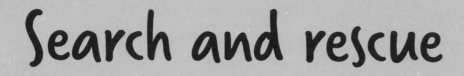

Dogs are very valuable members of any search and rescue team; they can track, locate, and get to places that are impossible for humans. They have been known to find people underwater, under collapsed buildings, and in avalanches, mudslides, and earthquakes.

19. Newfoundland (Canada)

These water-loving giants are the ultimate fisherman's friend. Not only did they help by drawing out their fishing nets but would rescue fishermen if they fell in the water. They have a natural instinct for water rescue, even if it means taking on rough ocean waves and powerful tides. This makes them an ideal and efficient lifeguard. In fact, a dog called Bilbo was a qualified lifeguard on Cornwall beaches.

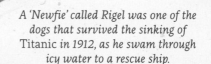

A 'Newfie' called Rigel was one of the dogs that survived the sinking of Titanic in 1912, as he swam through icy water to a rescue ship.

20. St Bernard (Switzerland)

The St Bernard is a fluffy canine equivalent of a snow plough, and it wasn't long before the monks who raised them in the snowy Alps realized their potential for mountain rescue and set up a hospice. Originally used as guard and companion dogs, St Bernards are able to find people in avalanches, trapped under metres of snow. One dog would run to alert the monks while the other used their huge paws to dig and their strength to pull a person out and keep them warm. A dog called Barry was especially skilled, saving between 40 and 100 people. In his honor, there is always a dog called Barry at the hospice, and the search and rescue dogs are often called 'Barry dogs'.

21. Airedale Terrier (United Kingdom)

With a vital message around their neck or packs of medicine strapped to their body, Airedale Terriers were often used to communicate over the battlefield or to help locate wounded soldiers during the World Wars. The Airedale Terrier made up a large percentage of the 20,000 pup paramedics that were referred to as mercy dogs.

Airedale Jack was one of the messenger dogs who ran through enemy fire during World War I with a message attached to his collar. He arrived just in time, saving a whole army base. For his bravery, Jack was awarded the Victoria Cross medal.

Most employable dogs

These dogs have no problem being popular. Intelligent, athletic, with a good sense of smell and an eagerness to work, they can be trained to do almost any job, achieving many 'firsts' in the canine working world.

22. German Shepherd (Germany)
No job is too small or task too challenging for this infamously versatile and intelligent breed. Police, military, search and rescue, detection, assistance... the list of jobs goes on and on. Shout out to these super Shepherds:

🐾 Buddy became the first seeing eye dog in 1928.

🐾 Gabi stopped a jaguar from escaping a zoo.

🐾 Mancs, a search and rescue dog, travelled all over the world because he was so good at finding people after earthquakes.

23. Labrador Retriever (Canada)
"Work hard, play hard … and chill" is this breed's motto. They like to play and LOVE water, but when they have a job to do they take it very seriously, which is why they are often bred to be guide dogs. The Labrador Retriever has been the most popular dog in the world since 1991, so they must be pretty awesome, but just in case you didn't believe the hype …

🐾 Favour became the first hearing dog for deaf people in 1982.

🐾 Assistance dog Endal understood over 100 verbal and signed commands, and could even use a cash machine.

🐾 Guide dogs Salty and Rosselle led their owners—and 30 other people—out of a burning building and down nearly 80 flights of stairs to safety.

🐾 Navy dog, Frida, rescued 52 people all over the world, all while wearing googles and boots.

If you have ever seen a dog wearing a special jacket, it is likely because they are doing a very important job. Here are just some of the ways assistance dogs help people in their everyday life.

RING! RING!

Guide dogs help those who are visually impaired to navigate the world around them. These jobs would include going to the shops or using public transport.

Hearing dogs are the ears for deaf people. They do the important job of alerting their owner to sounds like door bells, phones, or fire alarms.

Medical alert dogs are able to tell their owner if they need to take medication, are about to have a seizure, or should avoid certain foods.

Mobility assistance dogs are trained to make everyday tasks easier, such as opening doors, bringing items, and even loading the washing machine.

Support dogs are able to help people with autism by providing comfort and reducing stress.

Some dogs are even learning how to perform medical assistance, such as CPR!

Clever canines

On average, a dog is as smart as a two-year-old child and can understand around 150 words. Dog intelligence is measured by how easily they learn, problem solve, and communicate. By this standard, the Afghan doesn't rank too highly, but these are the breeds you want on your quiz team...

Some call me "genius," or "World's Smartest Dog," but my real name is Chaser and I know the names of over 1,000 objects.

24. Border Collie (England, Scotland)
First prize for smartest dog on the planet goes to ... the Border Collie! But the Collie's chart-topping skills don't end there. Not only are they the number one herding dog, but their amazing agility, obedience, and love for mental challenges means these dogs have been setting records all over the world—for skateboarding, dancing, and even balancing things on their head!

25. Doberman Pinscher (Germany)

This breed learns so quickly that it can pick up new tricks faster than you can say Doberman. Well, maybe not that quick, but they do learn up to five times faster than most other breeds, which is why they are a popular choice for the police and military. A top guard dog, this breed is good at recognizing friend from foe.

26. Poodle (Germany)

Mirror mirror on the wall, who's the prettiest pooch in the parlor? Poodles are known for their distinctive pom-pom hairdos, but they aren't too precious about their pretty perms when it comes to water. They are made for it! In fact, their name comes from the German word "Pudelin," meaning "to splash in water." With both brains and beauty, the Poodle comes in second place for intelligence.

27. Golden Retriever (Scotland)

No dog is happier to see you than the lovable Golden Retriever. They have bags of affection and love to make people happy. "Goldens" used as therapy dogs are known to sense the person who needs them the most. Some say if you give a Golden Retriever an egg, they will hold it in their mouth with the utmost gentleness and won't crack or drop it.

28. Weimaraner (Germany)

With a reputation of outsmarting their owners, the witty Weimaraner is no stranger to canine crimes. When you're as stealthy and nimble as a ninja, unlocking gates, cracking open crates, and stealing treats is simple. They are also known as the Gray Ghost, not just for their unusual silver-blue fur and piercing eyes, but because of their silent hunting style. They are so covert they even mask their own scent by rolling in something unpleasant, such as FOX POOP! Ugh!

Shhh, you never saw me.

Street smarts

In the hustle and bustle of a busy subway station, the last thing you would expect to see is a dog on its daily commute. Well, that is exactly what you could see in Moscow, Russia, where stray dogs have learned how to get on and off at their regular stops. Traveling from their homes in the suburbs to the crowded city center for food, these dogs have even learned to send certain dogs from the pack who were more successful at getting food.

Dogs around the world have been known to use buses on their own. A dog called Eclipse had her own bus pass, and regularly took herself to the park and returned home—just in time for dinner.

Drop me off at the park please, driver.

Play? Outside? Friend?

Talking dogs

Dogs communicate with their tails, body posture, and even by copying our facial expressions. They have 11 different ways of barking, from saying "hello" to "stay away!" But some dogs are learning to communicate with us by pressing special buttons programmed to say a specific word.

WOOF! I heard there's a dog who "talks" using buttons. With nearly 100 words to press, Bunny the dog is able to tell her owner what she wants to do and also express how she feels. I know what I'd ask for...
more treats please!

Do dogs have a sixth sense?

Did you know that dogs can predict the weather using their super smell, supersonic hearing, and finely-tuned fur? They can sense even the slightest shift in electric field, air pressure, or ground movement. Dogs have even been known to alert their humans to earthquakes, hurricanes, and tsunamis with enough time to get to safety.

We know dogs know how we are feeling by the way we smell, but do you think it's possible they know what we are going to do before we do it? Sounds crazy right? But studies have shown that some dogs know when we are coming home (even at an unexpected time), and can even tell if we do things on purpose or by accident. This has led to some people believing dogs and humans have such a strong connection that they are able to read our minds.

Therapy dogs

Animal-assisted therapy was pioneered by famous nurse Florence Nightingale, who believed it helped in her patients' recovery. We now see our furry friends helping in hospitals, schools, and lending a comforting paw in highly stressful situations. Here are the amazing ways therapy dogs work their magic.

How do dogs help?

When humans are around dogs, they release a chemical called oxytocin (also known as the "cuddle chemical") and show a reduction in cortisol, a stress hormone. Put simply, being with dogs makes us feel better.

Sigmund Freud and Jofi

Psychoanalyst Freud had his Chow Chow, Jofi, sit in on his therapy sessions. Freud believed Jofi was a good judge of character and calmed the patients. Jofi would also tell Freud when the session's time was up by getting up and yawning.

World first

A tiny Yorkshire Terrier called Smoky was one of the first therapy dogs. In World War II, she accompanied nurses on their rounds, spent time with injured soldiers, and entertained them with tricks.

Recovery and wellbeing

Many dogs support or help those in recovery from physical and mental traumas. These therapy dogs often have an incredible ability to sense and approach those who most need their help.

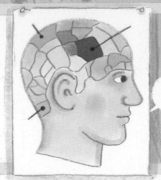

Crisis response and relief

At disaster sites where there are high levels of stress, some dogs work on search and rescue, while others provide comfort to victims, and even the emergency workers.

R.E.A.D.ing dogs

A dog does not judge, rush, or correct mistakes. They just listen. Which is why some dogs are being used to help children learn and enjoy reading. Reading Education Assistance Dogs help children who struggle with reading, by making it a more enjoyable and relaxing experience.

Companions

There are countless stories of dogs' unwavering faithfulness to their humans. Though some of these breeds also protect and hunt, many have always been bred for companionship. For these dogs, there is nothing better than to be by our side.

Did you know the Brussels Griffon was the inspiration for the Ewoks in Star Wars.

29. Papillon (Belgium, France)

The limelight-loving Papillon will do anything for a little attention. Luckily, they are incredibly smart so they know how to make sure your eyes are always on them, from doing tricks to gently fluttering their butterfly ears. Even when you might be on the toilet. Yeah, privacy isn't really their thing.

30. Volpino Italiano (Italy)

Parading along tile-floored palaces or trotting through dusty Tuscan farms, the "Little Fox" was the favored companion of Italian royalty as well as peasant farmers. The famous artist Michelangelo had several during his life and they kept him company in the four years it took him to paint the Sistine Chapel.

31. Maltese (Malta)

Eating out of gold dishes, wearing diamond necklaces, and even inheriting millions from their smitten owners, the Maltese is used to being spoiled and has a reputation for getting exactly what it wants. From sitting on the laps of ancient Egyptians and tucked under the dresses of empresses, to being cuddled and carried in handbags, the silky-haired Maltese has been a true comfort dog for centuries.

32. Dachshund (Germany)

The Dachshund is the smallest of the hounds, but has a big personality and an even bigger bark. Once used to tunnel into small holes to hunt badgers and rabbits, they still love to dig, though you're more likely to find these huggable hounds tucked up in your bed than in a burrow. Their short legs and long slender bodies earned them the nickname "sausage dogs."

A Dachshund called Waldi was the first ever Olympic mascot, created for the 1972 Munich Olympics. The marathon track was even plotted in the shape of a Dachshund.

Did someone say sausages?

33. Brussels Griffon (Belgium)

If you were catching a horse-drawn "taxi" in the 18th century, you'd likely be sharing a ride with a Brussels Griffon. As a coachman's companion and colleague, these dogs were as happy to sit on the long rides as they were to do the important job of ratting stables and protecting the horses.

34. French Bulldog (France, England)

Love to sing? Then the Frenchie could be your perfect doggy duet partner. With their yips, yaps, and gargles, they love to sing along to a tune. But don't scold them for singing off-key; Frenchies are incredibly sensitive to criticism and may go off in a huff. With their love for company, they are sure to jump back into your arms and wait for you to apologize.

Sadly, these loveable lap warmers have difficulty breathing because they have been bred to have very short noses. They are even banned from planes as it is too dangerous for them to fly.

National treasures

35. Keeshond (Netherlands)
Traveling leisurely along canals on a chilly fall day would be bliss for this foxy-faced fluff. Originally a boatman's companion and watchdog, these "Velcro" dogs just adore being with their human. So friendly they would greet a burglar with a joyful expression and a friendly lick, they earned the nickname "Smiling Dutchman," but not the reputation of a good guard dog.

36. Korean Jindo Dog (South Korea)
The Jindo is very important to the Korean people: they have protected status and even their own research institute! Those who arrive on Jindo Island are greeted by a statue of Baekgu, a dog who, as the story goes, was sold and taken over 180 miles away to be used as a police guard dog. But Baekgu escaped and, several months later, returned to her original owner. Baekgu's story of incredible loyalty has been made into movies, cartoons, and several books.

37. Coton de Tulear (Madagascar)
Little is known about how these dogs ended up in Madagascar, but the tale goes that they are descended from little white dogs that survived a pirate shipwreck and swam courageously to the shores of the island. For a long time, these cotton-coated canines were only allowed to be the companions of the wealthy. They are both the royal and national dog of Madagascar, and their fluffy faces even feature on their own Madagascan stamp.

Dogs around the world

As well as the millions of unique and marvelous mixes across the world there are over 400 recognizable breeds. When we know where different dogs come from we can begin to understand why they perform the jobs they do and why they may look a certain way. These breeds are often grouped into the categories below.

Hound – Traditionally used to help humans hunt, these dogs are equipped with awesome eyesight or a super sniffer.

Working – Some of the oldest breeds, the dogs in this group are large and strong with specific jobs like guarding or pulling sleds.

Pastoral – These super smart working breeds are used specifically for protecting and herding flocks.

Sporting – High-energy, alert dogs that excel at swimming and/or locating and retrieving items.

Terrier – With a love of digging and chasing, brave Terriers were originally used to hunt vermin.

Toy – These tiny lap-lovers are usually companion breeds.

Utility – A hugely diverse group in looks and personality that haven't been bred for any particular purpose.

Primitive This small group of perfect prick-eared pups have remained unchanged for thousands of years, evolving naturally and uninfluenced by other breeds.

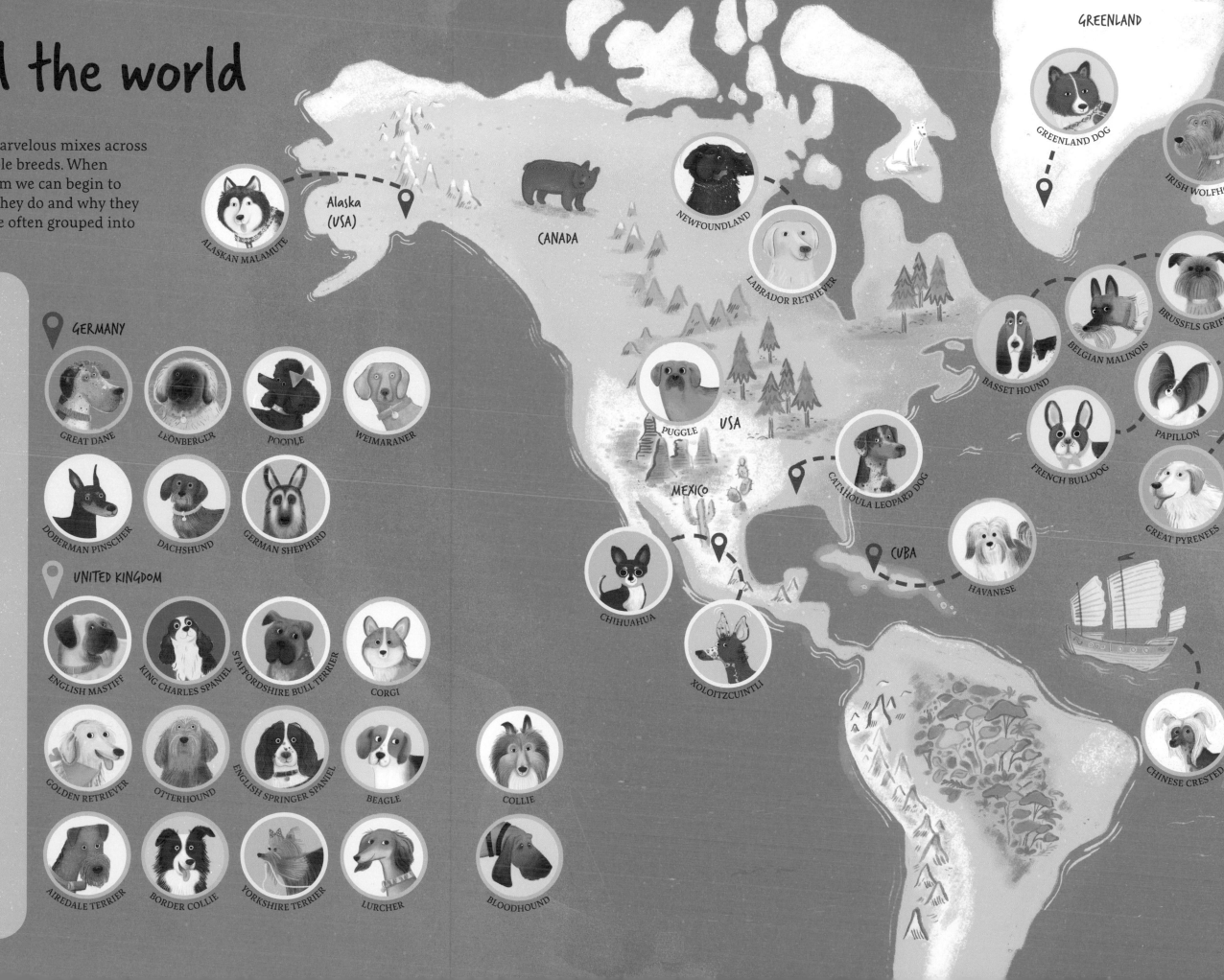

GREENLAND

GREENLAND DOG

IRISH WOLFHOUND

Alaska (USA)

ALASKAN MALAMUTE

CANADA

NEWFOUNDLAND

LABRADOR RETRIEVER

BASSET HOUND

BELGIAN MALINOIS

BRUSSELS GRIFFON

GERMANY

GREAT DANE

LEONBERGER

POODLE

WEIMARANER

DOBERMAN PINSCHER

DACHSHUND

GERMAN SHEPHERD

PUGGLE

USA

MEXICO

CATAHOULA LEOPARD DOG

FRENCH BULLDOG

PAPILLON

CUBA

HAVANESE

GREAT PYRENEES

UNITED KINGDOM

ENGLISH MASTIFF

KING CHARLES SPANIEL

STAFFORDSHIRE BULL TERRIER

CORGI

CHIHUAHUA

XOLOITZCUINTLI

GOLDEN RETRIEVER

OTTERHOUND

ENGLISH SPRINGER SPANIEL

BEAGLE

COLLIE

CHINESE CRESTED

AIREDALE TERRIER

BORDER COLLIE

YORKSHIRE TERRIER

LURCHER

BLOODHOUND

38. Taigan (Kyrgyzstan)

This top secret sight hound is considered so special that even its origin is hidden in folklore. The local people say the first Taigan hatched from a mythical bird egg and chased wolves away from the town, saving the people and their cattle.

Traditionally, these dogs were only ever given as a wedding gift, never sold, and they are still as highly regarded. Even today, an outsider must get permission to see one and they are celebrated with annual festivals.

39. Havanese (Cuba)

This Cuban canine is incredibly curious and clever, and loves nothing more than to explore the world, preferably bouncing by the side of their human. That is except their bizarre fascination with anything paper, often going out of their way to find some in pursuit of hours of shredding pleasure.

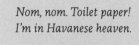

Nom, nom. Toilet paper! I'm in Havanese heaven.

Dogs with odd jobs

Throughout history dogs have been used to perform some pretty peculiar tasks. Take a look at some of the interesting jobs dogs have done...

Throughout the Victorian era in the United Kingdom, coin-collecting canines were a common sight in every large railroad station. With tin boxes strapped to their backs, the dogs collected money for all sorts of good causes, because it was believed people gave far more generously to the dogs than to people.

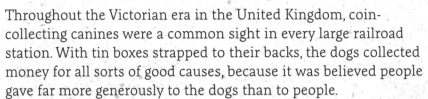

I'm Laddie from Waterloo Station. I raised £5,000 ($6,250) for orphans—the equivalent of £100,000 ($125,000) today.

Jax was an official stamp licker for a post office.

Nati, a Jack Russel mix, is a surrogate mom to orphaned animals in Africa—often those who become twice her size! Hyenas, monkeys, jackals, baboons, and cheetahs: whatever their species, Nati looks after them, grooming and acting as a playmate, until they can be safely released back into the wild.

NORWEGIAN LUNDEHUND

SWEDISH VALLHUND

NORWAY

FINLAND

SWEDEN

FINNISH LAPPHUND

RUSSIA

SAMOYED

KEESHOND

NETHERLANDS

KOMONDOR

PEKINGESE

CHOW CHOW

SHAR PEI

BORZOI

SIBERIAN HUSKY

BELGIUM

CESKY TERRIER

CZECHIA

FRANCE

SWITZERLAND

HUNGARY

CROATIA

MUDI

KUVASZ

TAIGAN

KYRGYZSTAN

CHINA

ITALY

SOUTH KOREA

JAPAN

AKITA INU

SPAIN

ST. BERNARD

MALTA

DALMATIAN

TURKEY

CAUCASIAN SHEPHERD

AFGHANISTAN

TIBETAN MASTIFF

TIBETAN TERRIER

BERGAMASCO

NEAPOLITAN MASTIFF

MAREMMA

BERNESE MOUNTAIN DOG

MALTESE

ÇATALBURUN

SALUKI

INDIA

AFGHAN HOUND

JINDO

LAGOTTO ROMAGNOLO

VOLPINO ITALIANO

WEST AFRICA

CAMBODIA

CAMBODIAN RAZORBACK

NEW GUINEA SINGING DOG

AZAWAKH

DEMOCRATIC
REPUBLIC OF CONGO

BASENJI

MADAGASCAR

BAKHARWAL

MALAYSIA

PAPUA NEW
GUINEA

AUSTRALIAN CATTLE DOG

RHODESIAN RIDGEBACK

COTON DE TULEAR

TELOMIAN

NEW ZEALAND

ZIMBABWE

AUSTRALIA

LABRADOODLE

A Jack Russell called Tillamook was regarded as one of the best dog artists. She used her teeth and claws to "draw."

I sold that one for more than $2,000.

Wearing a special suit that tracks a dog's movement, game developers can make the movement of dogs more realistic in video games.

Bosco won an election with his slogan *A bone in every dish, a cat in every tree, and a fire hydrant on every corner*, beating two human candidates to become honorary Mayor of Sunol, California, from 1981–1994.

Rescue dogs have been trained to be ball dogs during Brazillian tennis tournaments. Not only do the dogs enjoy it, but they raise awareness of the dog shelters and promote adoption.

Dogs are used to chase birds and be airport runway clearers, making sure both the wildlife and flight paths are safe.

This is my dream job!

Dogs like Lila the Labrador are doing their part for the environment. Lila moved on from diving for lobsters to working with 4Ocean, cleaning the ocean of plastic off the coast of Florida.

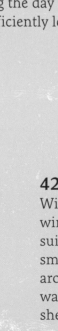

Snow dogs

For thousands of years, people who migrated north of the Arctic Circle have been using dogs, not only to herd reindeer but to perform another vital role: transport. Because of the dogs, goods and people could travel over vast distances, enabling communication between communities. Without these incredible dogs, these civilizations are unlikely to have survived.

40. Greenland (Greenland)
The Greenland Dog is a true sledding superpower. With a thick, oily coat, this dog can work at a teeth chattering –68°F! The dogs are said to have played a vital role in both the expeditions to reach the North Pole and the capturing of the South Pole by famous explorer, Roald Amundsen, in 1911.

41. Finnish Lapphund (Finland)
Lapphunds are certainly no lapdog. They actually get their name from the Sámi people who lived for thousands of years in an area that was once called Lapland. On extremely cold nights the dogs and people would huddle together to stay warm, but during the day this feisty dog would herd fast-moving reindeer with an efficiently loud, squeaky bark.

42. Samoyed (Russia)
With fur as white as snow and as thick as a winter blanket, this reindeer herder is perfectly suited to the iciest of climates. Its infamous smile prevents drooling and icicles forming around its mouth. A Samoyed's fur is so warm and soft, it is even collected when shed to make sweaters.

As civilizations expanded, the desire to deliver packages and letters across this remote and vast land increased. Malamutes worked as important employees of the Alaskan postal service until 1963, and are the official state dog of Alaska.

Woo wooo!

43. Alaskan Malamute (USA)

There aren't many dogs brave enough to come face-to-face with a toothy polar bear, but for the largest and strongest of all the sled dogs, this was not an unusual task. Originally Mahlemut tribes used them to pull heavy sleds loaded with food and camping items. These abilities made them in extremely high demand during the Klondike Gold Rush of 1896, where they were used to haul heavy precious metal through the mountain passes.

Most snow dog breeds are very old breeds that still have their wolflike looks.

We love to work as a team, but just one of us can pull twice as much as a horse.

44. Siberian Husky (Siberia, Russia)

Huskies are often mistaken for Malamutes, even though they are smaller. But a Husky can have brown eyes, pale blue eyes, or one of each, and are mainly used for transporting lighter loads at a much quicker speed.

The Great Mercy Race

The importance of sled dogs for transport was highlighted in Alaska in 1925, when a deadly infection threatened the lives of those in a remote town called Nome. Trains were out of action in the harsh winter conditions, and delivery of medicine would have been impossible without Siberian Huskies. A relay of 20 mushers and 150 dogs traveled 674 miles through blizzards and hurricane-force winds for five and a half days. They saved countless lives.

I'm Balto. I became famous for delivering precious medicine, and you can find a statue of me in Central Park, New York.

I'm Togo. My pack and musher, Seppala, traveled the longest part of the journey— 260 miles!

ALASKA

Mushing

Powered snowmobiles means sled dogs are no longer needed for transport. But these pack dogs still love this form of exercise and continue sledding with their humans as a hobby or competitively. This is called mushing. The Great Mercy Race helped shape one of the most iconic sled dog races—the Iditarod Trail. It's the toughest and most famous sled dog race in the world, taking eight to ten days to complete.

In places without snow, some people exercise their highly energetic huskies in a less demanding version of mushing, called bikejoring.

I can run at a speed of 30 miles per hour.

Competitive canines

Sports allow dogs to display their natural abilities. They challenge them mentally and strengthen the bond between dog and human.

Doggy dancing is much more than wagging a tail to a beat, it is a sport of outstanding obedience, where dog and human perform a dramatic heelwork routine of extraordinary tricks set to music.

When it comes to disc dog (or Frisbee dog), either the most impressive catch (usually consisting of leaps and flips) or catch over the longest distance wins.

Sailor caught a Frisbee at almost 330 feet away.

Fast and fearless dogs sprint down a boardwalk and leap over water as far as they can to retrieve a toy in a sport called dock diving. Legendary dog, Sounders, won the world record for farthest jump (by a dog) in 2022, with a whopping 36.48 feet. That's longer than a school bus!

Sheepdog trials are a test of a dog's herding skills. Listening to commands, the dog must guide sheep though an obstacle course and into a pen as accurately as possible.

We're the fastest dogs on wheels!

I hold the record for longest wave surfed by a dog—over 350 feet.

Dogs like Abbie give a whole new meaning to the term "doggy paddle." She was the first surfing dog in the International Surfing Hall of Fame.

On a dog agility course, the human directs the dog through an obstacle course of tight turns, tunnels, and seesaws in a race against the clock.

Shadow holds the deepest scuba dive at 13 feet, while Bellybutton was able to deep dive over 20 feet.

My name is Verb, and I completed an agility course in just 31.3 seconds.

Dog discoveries

Classical conditioning

Have you ever trained a dog to "Sit!," "Stay!," or "Roll over!" by using treats? If so, you've used classical conditioning. This theory of learning was discovered by Ivan Pavlov and his dogs in 1897, when he realized that he could get his dogs to associate the sound of a bell with food. This experiment was a huge psychological breakthrough at the time, teaching us a lot about behavior and learning through association. It is still used today in behavioral therapy and learning.

The Lascaux cave

One day in 1940, adventurous dog, Robot, found himself in a cave. But it was no ordinary cave. The walls were magnificently decorated with detailed painted figures. In fact, Robot had discovered one of the earliest examples of prehistoric artwork, which was more than 17,000 years old! The cave taught scientists about prehistoric culture and the history of art.

I'm a real life Indiana Bones.

Doggy doubles

In 1996, Dolly the sheep became the very first cloned mammal. But the first cloned dog, in 2005, was an Afghan Hound called Snuppy, born in Seoul, South Korea. Scientists discovered that while looks can be replicated, a personality can never be cloned.

Air pollution monitor

Bagheera raises awareness of air pollution levels by wearing a data collecting device around her neck while on her walks. Dogs like Baggy have also highlighted the health risks people and pets face by using aerosols in our homes.

Bionic dog

Naki'o was the first dog that needed four bionic legs. The research and engineering that went into making his amazing legs played a significant part in the development of pet prosthetics.

Insulin

Millions of people around the world with Type 1 diabetes owe their lives to a discovery made possible by a dog called Marjorie. In 1921, scientists Frederick Banting and Charles Best discovered that insulin produced in a healthy pancreas was needed to control glucose in the blood. Marjorie was chosen to have her pancreas removed and was successfully given insulin as a treatment. Though Marjorie didn't live long after this procedure, her sacrifice was not in vain, as scientists went on to develop the life-saving insulin drug used today.

Dog-stronomy

There are more than 80 constellations in the night sky, but the brightest star of all is called Sirius (or the Dog Star), and is part of Canis Major, also known as the Great Dog Constellation.

Velcro

One day in 1941, after a long walk through woodlands and fields, Milka's fur was covered in prickly burdock burrs. Struck by the way these seed heads stuck to her fur, her engineer owner was (after much research) able to develop Velcro®.

NASA started using Velcro's grippy hook and loop mechanism and its popularity soared. They used it to stop items floating around, securing pockets, devices, and cuffs on spacesuits. Now we use it for closing bags or fastening shoes.

There's a little piece of Velcro in my helmet that I use to scratch my nose.

Dogonauts

Before humans went to space, several national space programs tested the effects of this unfamiliar journey on other animals. These included insects, birds, monkeys, and dogs.

While the U.S. mainly worked with monkeys, the Soviet space program used dogs for space flights during the 1950s and 1960s. They were all female strays, chosen because scientists thought they'd cope with stress better than people's pets.

However, the mission of Laika—the first dog to orbit Earth—sparked a debate across the globe on the mistreatment of animals, and scientific animal testing in general.

My name is Laika. I was the first dog to orbit Earth in 1957.

Belka & Strelka

Belka (Whitey) and Strelka (Little Arrow) were the first dogonauts to orbit and return safely to Earth. One of Strelka's six puppies, called Pushinka, was sent to America to live with President John F. Kennedy.

Zvyozdochka

Zvyozdochka (Little Star) was named by cosmonaut Yuri Gagarin. Zvyozdochka's successful flight gave Gagarin the confidence he needed to become the first human in space on April 12, 1961.

Huge hounds

The record for the longest dog tail goes to Irish Wolfhound, Keon—31 inches.

45. Leonberger (Germany)
65–110 lbs • 25–31 in.

This bushy-tailed beauty is the result of one man's vision to create a dog version of the lion on Leonburg's coat of arms. They were then gifted to European royalty. In size, the Leonberger follows in the large, fluffy footsteps of its cousins, the St. Bernard, Pyrenees, and the Newfoundland. They were used for carting, particularly during World War I, to deliver ammunition to the battlefield.

46. Irish Wolfhound (Ireland)
88–110 lbs • 28–34 in.

The lovable long-legged Irish Wolfhound is the tallest dog breed in the world. They are fast but lazy, and adored by their humans. One owner's love for their Irish Wolfhound may have even started a war in the 12th century, when they refused to trade their dog, Aibe, for 4,000 cows.

The smallest dog ever was a Chihuahua called Milly. She was four inches tall and as light as this book.

Chihuahua for scale

47. Great Dane (Germany)
100–120 lbs • 28–30 in.

The Great Dane is the largest lapdog. Despite their massive size, their favorite place to sit is on your lap or cuddled up on the couch. Unsurprisingly, these gentle giants also have some pretty big paws—about the same size as an average man's hand!

The tallest dog ever was a Great Dane called Zeus, at three feet eight inches. When standing on two legs he was over six feet tall!

Cartoon character Scooby-Doo is a Great Dane like me.

48. Neapolitan Mastiff (Italy)
110–155 lbs • 23–30 in.

No, this dog isn't melting! Originally bred in the Roman Empire to be used in combat, their intimidating looks, wrinkles and folds protected them in battle. They're gentle, affectionate dogs, though when they shake their head you may get showered in slobber.

Mastiffs have the largest litters of any breed. The largest ever litter was that of Tia, who had 24 puppies.

49. English Mastiff (England)
155–220 lbs • 28–35 in.

These muscular Mastiffs are the most giant of all breeds originating from ancient Roman war dogs. The largest ever dog was called Zorba, who weighed in at a whooping 340 pounds. That's the same as *three* Great Danes.

Tiny toys and terriers

50. Chihuahua (Mexico)

"Chihuahua" (pronounched Chiwawah) is one of the most frequently misspelled words; they are also one of the world's smallest breeds, but they don't let that hold them back. Chihuahuas have big brains, big personalities, and bags of courage, often thinking they are much bigger than they are. One pint-sized Chihuahua was even known to bravely fight off a rattlesnake to protect a baby.

They also play a huge role in the celebration of Mexican heritage, often being dressed up for Cinco de Mayo festivities and raced in the "Running of the Chihuahuas." Back in 1887, a famous opera singer was gifted a large bouquet of flowers hiding a tiny Chihuahua puppy that popped out—surprise!

51. Cesky Terrier (Czechia)

The Cesky Terrier features a particularly impressive mustache and bushy eyebrows —something they're said to share with the man who created the breed. Like other Terriers, such as the Bedlington and Kerry Blue, they are born with black fur, which lightens into shades of gray and blue after a year or two.

52. Yorkshire Terrier (England)

Regularly seen chasing the biggest dogs around the park, the Yorkshire Terrier has the courage of a Mastiff and the belief they are the size of a Great Dane. However, within this tiny package is an agile and energetic hunter. Throughout the 19th century they were used to catch mice and rats in clothing mills, since they were perfectly sized to weave in between looms and sewing machines. It was often joked that their time in the textile industry is the reason for their magnificent long hair, "fine as spun gold."

53. Staffordshire Bull Terrier (England)

Afraid of spiders? No way! The strong Staffordshire Bull Terrier is not afraid of anything and is always ready to protect its family. They were once used as fighting dogs, but with good training they also have a very patient and calming presence and were often called "nanny dogs," after their caring nature.

54. Tibetan Terrier (Tibet)

Draw back the curtains of the Tibetan's hair and you'll soon realize this dog isn't a Terrier at all—they were incorrectly named because of their appearance. They were raised as companions to Buddhist monks and mountain herders 2,000 years ago, who believed the dog to be a good luck charm.

Royal dogs

55. Kuvasz (Hungary)

The Kuvasz had an incredible journey from humble guardian of flocks to the king's most trusted ally. Famed for their legendary guardian skills, the Kuvasz soon became popular as hunting companions and lived up to the meaning of their name: "armed guard of the nobility." Gifted from royalty to royalty, some kings say they trusted their dogs more than they trusted the people around them.

56. Cavalier King Charles Spaniel (England)

King Charles II loved this friendly breed so much it was later named in his honor. The breed comes in different colors all with equally regal names. Prince Charles (tricolor), King Charles (black and tan), Ruby (mahogany), and Blenheim (chestnut and white), named after a battle that was won by the Duke of Marlborough. It is thought that the Cavalier is the furthest removed physically from their wolf ancestors.

57. Pembroke Welsh Corgi (Wales)

Corgis and Queen Elizabeth II of England went hand in hand. Since receiving her first Pembroke Welsh Corgi in 1933, the Queen had over 30 of them in her lifetime. At one point there were so many parading about the palace that they were likened to a "moving carpet."

The pattern on some Corgis' coats looks like a saddle and harness, and many people used to tell children that Corgis are enchanted dogs, ridden by elves at night.

All of our meals were cooked by the royal chef.

58. Borzoi (Russia)

You can easily imagine the elegant Borzoi with their silky coat, feathery tails, and tall, slender frame gliding into a gold palace ballroom. But in reality, they were bred as fast (their name means swift), powerful hunting dogs that could survive brutal Russian winters. They became extremely popular with the czars and aristocracy, who used them to hunt in large groups and even to pin down wolves.

59. Pekingese (China)

Resembling a fluffy slipper more than it does the large cat from which it gets its nickname "Lion Dog," the Pekingese were a favorite of Chinese emperors and were certainly treated like royalty themselves. Not only were they carried around in the warmth of robe sleeves, but they had their own servants. Commoners had to bow before them, and theft of one would even mean death.

So why are they called lion dogs? One ancient tale goes that a lion was so in love with a monkey that he asked the gods to make them the same size, while retaining his lion heart. The first Pekingese was the result.

Howl of fame

From hero hounds to most popular dog, canines on camera to mascot mutts. Roll out the red carpet and call the puparazzi because here comes a rather fantastic pack of pooches.

Munito

Munito started off in France, in 1817, as a domino-playing dog, but went on to become one of the most famous performing pooches in history. Touring all of Europe, crowds watched in amazement as "The Wonderful Dog" seemed to calculate sums, perform tricks, understand and spell out words in French or English—and even read people's palms.

Most decorated war dog.

The ancient city—Peritas, was named after this dog.

Snoopy is one of the world's most famous cartoon dogs.

With over 10 million followers, Jiff was one of the most popular dogs on the internet, and the fastest dog on two legs.

Rin Tin Tin

With lead roles in 27 films, Rin Tin Tin found global fame and was awarded a star on the Hollywood Walk of Fame. Without the huge success of Rin Tin Tin's film's, Warner Bros. film studio wouldn't exist today, and the German Shepherd breed probably wouldn't have become so popular.

Nipper is the face of
His Master's Voice (HMV
Records Company).

Hachikō is known for
being one of the most
faithful dogs of all time.

Kratu

Remarkable rescue dog, Kratu, went viral after his cheeky agility
performances at Crufts Dog Show in 2017–20. In between zoomies
he played peek-a-boo in the tunnels, and even stole a pole from the
course. Kratu has become an ambassa-dog for international dog
charities, raising awareness of animal welfare, support dogs, and
the benefits of rescuing stray and abandoned dogs.

Masterpiece was an incredibly
famous supermodel dog in the 1950s.
He had his own bodyguard, beautician,
and traveling companion. One day he
disappeared without a trace, and the case
of "missing Masterpiece" is still a mystery.

Tika

From feather boas and
chunky knit sweaters to
glamorous ball gowns,
this tiny Italian Greyhound
has more outfits than most
people. She is not only a
fashion icon but, through
her large social media fame,
raises awareness and funds
for LGBTQ+ charities.

MASTERPIECE

Swansea Jack

People aren't usually named after dogs.
But Swansea Jack became such a legend
that it is said many children were named
in his honor. Swansea Jack was a hero
for saving 27 people and several puppies
from drowning over the years. Jack even
had his own song and won many awards
for his bravery.

Fascinating features

60. Basset Hound (France)

The Basset Hound is a superior sniffing machine! Every part of its body is designed to make it one of the best scent hounds around. Its short legs mean its nose is low to the ground, while its impressively long, floppy ears help draw up scent. The flap of skin under its chin, called a dewlap, helps to hold the scent near the nose. Its sense of smell is bested only by the Bloodhound.

61. Çatalburun (Turkey)

To say the Çatalburun (meaning "splitnose") is a rare breed is almost an understatement. With only 200 said to exist, it's very likely you will have never even heard of them, let alone met one. They are barely seen outside of their home city of Tarsus, and inbreeding is likely the cause of its bizarre-looking nose. Though some say it improves the dog's sense of smell, there is little evidence to say this is true.

There's a Xolo called Dante in the Disney/Pixar movie, Coco.

62. Xoloitzcuinti (Mexico)

Pronounced *show-low-eats-**queent**-ly*, this striking (almost) hairless dog was worshipped by the Aztecs, who named it after their god of lightning and death, Xolotl. They believed the dogs would guard the living and guide the souls of the dead to the Underworld. When not on mythical guide duty, Xolos love to snuggle up to you; their bodies are so toasty warm, they feel like living hot water bottles!

63. Catahoula Leopard Dog (USA)

Animals that can climb trees: squirrels, cats, monkeys ...
Catahoula Leopard Dogs? Yes, thats right, the Catahoula's
boundless energy, determination, and agility means they
have a highly unusual ability to climb trees. They are
no doubt aided by their large webbed feet, which also
help them wade through the Louisiana swamps. The
Catahoula often have a uniquely dappled coat (a bit like a
leopard) and their eyes come in a variety of colors.

Oops, I didn't think about the getting down part.

64. Shar Pei (China)

With more wrinkles than your grandpa and a harsh
"sandpaper" coat, the Shar Pei is certainly a striking-looking
dog. Their bristly coat and thick, saggy skin acted like body
armor against attack, back when they were used as hunting and
fighting dogs.

The Shar Pei is one of the few breeds (along with the Chow
Chow and Telomian) that have a distinctive blue tongue. Folk
tales say that back when the world was created they licked up
the little pieces of blue sky that fell down to Earth, and stars
were put in their place.

Now, that's what I call a downward facing dog.

65. Norwegian Lundehund (Norway)

If dogs did gymnastics, then this cliff-climbing
canine would be the champion. No other breed
comes close to the Lundehund's full-body
flexibility. Originally used to hunt Puffins along
the Norwegian coast, it is the only breed in the
world to have developed both a sixth toe
for grip and the ability to open and close
their ears to protect against water
and dirt.

Fancy fur

66. Komondor (Hungary)

This Hungarian sheepdog's moplike appearance is down to the many cords that make up its thick white coat. It blends in perfectly with the flocks of curly-haired sheep it is raised to protect, and the thick cords also protect the dog from the attacks of predators, such as wolves. It takes washing to maintain the pure white color of the Komondor's coat, and since it's so heavy it can take up to three days to dry.

67. Bergamasco (Italy, Iran)

Just like a Roman gladiator, the Bergamasco wears layers of "armor" to protect itself. These three flat blankets of texture, called "dog" (soft hair), "goat" (coarse hair), and "wool" (fleece) cover the whole body, creating warmth, camouflage and extra protection against weather and injury. And let's not forget their extraordinarily long eyelashes. They look fantastic, but also keep hair out of the dog's eyes and protect them from snow blindness.

68. Rhodesian Ridgeback
(South Africa, Zimbabwe)

Only three breeds in the world have a distinctive ridge along their back, formed by a stripe of hair growing in the opposite direction to the rest of the coat. Rhodesian Ridgebacks were considered braver than other dogs, able to corner and hold off lions until hunters could arrive, which gave them the nickname, "African Lion Dog." Though this watchful, quiet breed would probably rather go on a nice lion-free walk with you.

69. Cambodian Razorback
(Cambodia)

You would expect a dog living in such a hot climate to have short hair, but this rain forest rebel has a long thick coat, bushy tail and unmissable two-inch-long streak of spiked hair down its spine.

Hairless

Powderpuff

Can you believe a dog like me won "World's Ugliest Dog" ten times?

70. Chinese Crested (Africa, Mexico)

Though some people consider the breed cute and others ugly, there is no denying both the Hairless and the silky "Powderpuff" types are pretty eye-catching. Although the name suggests they originated in China, they likely came from Africa or Mexico, traded at ports by traveling Chinese ships, on which they gave sailors companionship and as acted as rat catchers.

71. Dalmatian (Croatia)

Like a splattering of paint on a blank canvas, the Dalmatian's coat is unique. In fact, the puppies are born white, only starting to develop their spectacular spotty coats after three weeks. Known as the "Spotted Coach Dog," throughout history this breed has run alongside wagons, carriages, and even fire trucks pulled by horses. They courageously cleared crowds and guarded the horses to make sure they weren't spooked by the fire. As a nod to the Dalmatian's past, this "Fire House" dog has become a mascot for many fire stations across America.

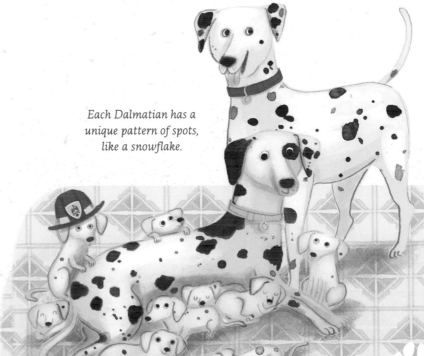

Each Dalmatian has a unique pattern of spots, like a snowflake.

Rare dogs

72. Otterhound (United Kingdom)
The Otterhound is considered one of the most endangered dogs in the world, which is hard to understand since they are such bouncy, happy dogs. They were once used to track otters, using their large webbed paws to wade through mud and water. When people stopped hunting otters this job was no longer needed, so the number of Otterhounds sadly declined.

It's raining cats and dogs and I almost stepped in a poodle.

73. Azawakh (West Africa)
The tall, long-legged Azawakh is super lean and athletic. With impressive speed, hunting skills, and intelligence, Azawaks were used to guard nomadic tribes and hunt hares and gazelle. In the desert heat, the Azawakh keeps cool by digging holes to lie in, but any lucky owners of this expensive breed will know how much they hate going out in the cold or the rain.

74. Swedish Vallhund (Sweden)
With the nickname "Viking dog," this dog probably isn't quite what you'd imagine. But despite its short legs and sassy Corgi-like waddle, the breed was a firm favorite with Vikings as a fantastic herding dog, driving their cattle with boundless energy. In the 1940s they almost became extinct, but because of the dog's versatile nature they are beginning to gain popularity.

75. Lagotto Romagnolo (Italy)

This perfectly permed pooch is said to be the first ever "water dog." Its tight, oily curls make its coat water resistant, meaning it can swim to retrieve game (hunted birds) in the water. But when the lakes of Romagna were drained, these dogs lost their jobs. Luckily their scent skills and love of mental exercise provided them with one job that saved them from extinction: truffle snuffling.

The world's largest white truffle was discovered by a Lagotto Romagnolo in 2014. The prized fungi sold for $61,250.

76. Telomian (Malaysia)

Having been raised with the indigenous people who lived in stilt houses, the Telomian has developed a pretty unique skill. After a hard day protecting their family from the tropical creepy-crawlies below, the Telomian would have to climb ladders back up to their home. This resulted in them developing superbly strong grip. Now they can hold objects, hang onto branches, and open doors. So don't forget to lock your doors —a Telomian might just let themselves in.

77. New Guinea Singing Dog (New Guinea)

This breed's loud, melodic fusion of wolf howl and whale song may not be popular with your neighbors, but with a wide vocal range, no other dog can give such a unique operatic performance. With only an estimated 200 dogs living in homes and in sanctuaries, it is believed this foxlike, primitive breed could be the rarest in the world.

Crossed canines

78. Puggle (USA)

You will know if this Pug/Beagle cross is in your home. Not only will you and everything you own be covered in their short spiky hair, but you'll probably also hear their wall-vibrating snore from the next room. They are cute, bursting with character, and love nothing more than being with their human companion. So when they are asleep it's likely they're dreaming of you.

79. Labradoodle (Australia)

A Labrador mixed with a Poodle may look like a big piece of fried chicken or a cute teddy bear. But whichever way you look at it, the breed was not intended to be the furry fashion accessory it is today. The original aim was to be a non-shedding guide dog for blind allergy sufferers. Through its popularity as a bouncy, intelligent breed with oodles of energy, this doodle dog became a trend setter, sparking the "designer" dog movement.

80. Lurcher (United Kingdom)

Can you believe that all of these dogs are actually the same breed? A mix of one or more sight hounds (Greyhound, Saluki, Wolfhound, etc) with a herding or terrier breed is called a Lurcher, and no two are the same—in looks or in character. But what they all have in common is the love of a good squirrel chase and long leisurely sofa snoozes. The name Lurcher comes from the words "lurch" and "lurk," presumably from their speedy and stealthy hunting style, or arguably their ability to steal an hour here and there for extra nap time. These classic couch potatoes can sleep up to 18 hours a day.

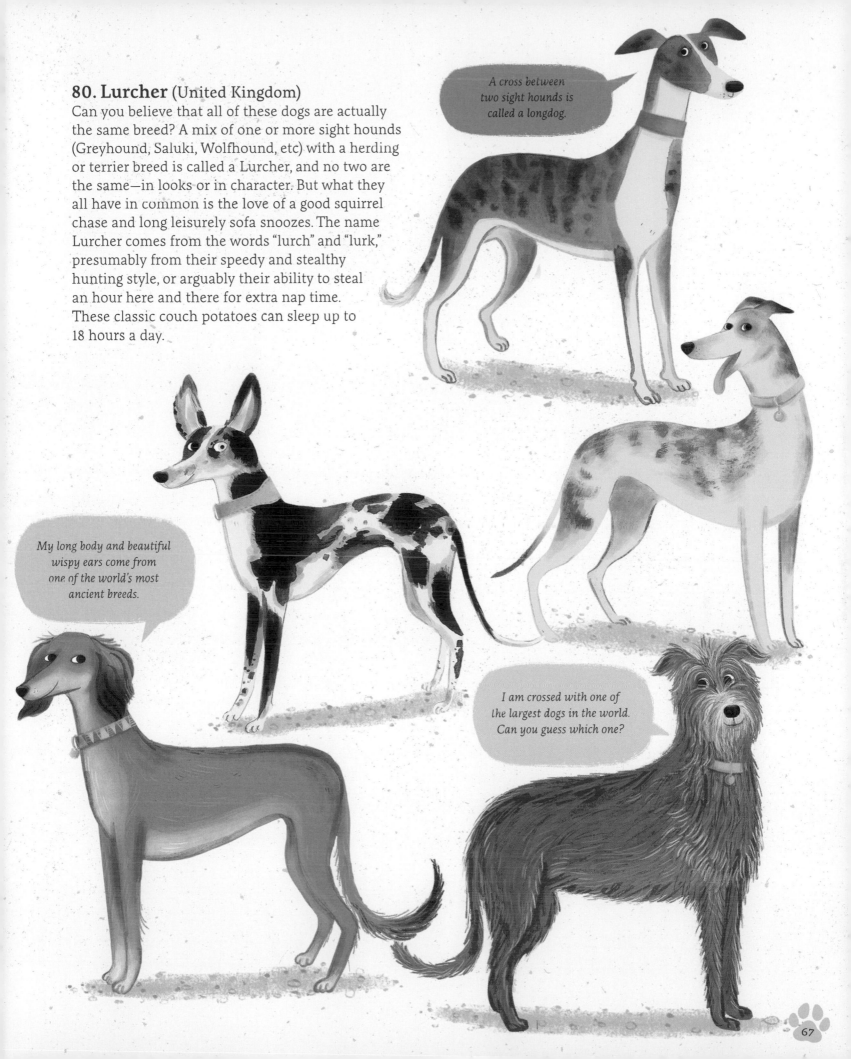

A cross between two sight hounds is called a longdog.

My long body and beautiful wispy ears come from one of the world's most ancient breeds.

I am crossed with one of the largest dogs in the world. Can you guess which one?

Marvelous mixes

Most of the dogs in the world are actually a muddle of multiple breeds. These dogs have less distinctive features, so it can be a real puzzle to figure out which breeds make up these marvelous mixes. The only way we can know for sure is by studying their DNA, but sometimes with a little doggy detective work we can find some clues by looking at these dogs from the top of their ears to the tip of their tails.

Face facts
There are three dog head shapes:

Dolichocephalic
A long, narrow face, such as Saluki, Borzoi, Poodle.

Mesaticephalic
A square shaped face, such as Cocker Spaniel, Labrador Retriever.

Brachycephalic
A short, flat face, such as Bulldog breeds, Pekingese.

Ears up!
There are 12 types of dog ear shapes, from sticky-uppy to flappy or droopy. Those with upright ears, like German Shepherds, have the best hearing, and large ears help dogs like French Bulldogs keep cool.

Ears with a slight bend, like those on a Border Collie, help them judge direction and distance of sound. They help dogs like the Greyhound to be more streamlined.

Prick ears

Bat-eared

Semi-prick

Rose

Its all in the (de)tails

Dogs use their tails for movement, balance, and communication. But they can also help us to identify certain breeds.

Sickle

These are often seen in Spitz dogs, such as Malamutes. In cold weather, their tail keeps their nose warm while they sleep.

Otter

Water dogs like Labrador Retrievers and Otterhounds have a thick tail to use as a rudder when swimming.

Coat clues

Wiry - Many terrier breeds have a wiry coat to keep out dirt and water.

Smooth - Commonly seen on sleek and speedy sight hounds.

Double - Often seen in outdoor working breeds for insulation.

Curly - Could indicate a water retrieving breed. Air trapped between curls helps keep them afloat.

Saber

A low tail is often seen in herding breeds, such as German Shepherds, Collies, Belgian Malinois. It gives them awesome balance.

Many dogs originally bred for pest control, such as Jack Russell and Brussels Griffon, have flapped ears to keep out dirt and bugs.

Retrievers and hunting hounds tend to have ears that fall downward to focus on scent over sound and protect water dog ears from water.

Carrot/whip

A shorter (carrot) tail is common in terrier breeds, while a longer (whip) tail helps dogs like Wolfhounds steer and brake during exciting chases.

Button

V-shaped

Drop

Fun facts

Dog days

🐾 You can celebrate International Dog Day on August 26 every year.

🐾 In Nepal, there is a five day festival. One of these days, Kukur Tihar, or "day of the dogs" celebrates all dogs with offerings of food and flower garlands.

🐾 "Dog days" are the days when Sirius, the Dog Star, is most visible in the sky.

🐾 A "three dog night" means it's going to be a cold night, so you will need to cuddle up with at least three of your furry friends to keep warm!

Did you know dogs' favorite music tends to be reggae and soft rock?

Top dogs

Superior sprinters: Greyhounds at 45 miles per hour.
Longest licker: Brandy the Boxer had a 17-inch-long tongue. That's as long as a giraffe's.
Biggest bark: Golden Retrievers at 113 decibels. That's as loud as a rock concert.
Longest dog conga: 14 dogs.
World's oldest dog: Bobi, over 30 years old.

Patriotic pooches

🐾 Purple poppies are worn to remember animals who served in wars.

🐾 Military I.D. tags are inspired by dog tags, which gives them their nickname.

🐾 A Great Dane called Juliana once defused a bomb by peeing on it, and was awarded a Blue Cross medal.

Did you know dogs can only see in shades of blue and yellow?

The scoop on poop

🐾 To find the perfect pooping place, dogs align themselves with the Earth's magnetic field along a north-south line.

🐾 Sometimes dogs will roll in stinky stuff as a way to tell their dog friends they found something cool.

🐾 A set of traffic lights in Japan was such a popular peeing place for pups that it collapsed!

Bowwow!!
That's one fast dog.

Index